PRESENTED TO:

_____

FROM:

_____

DATE:

_____

God's Word
FOR ME
BIBLE STORYBOOK

"Love the Lord your God. Love him with all your heart, all your soul, all your mind, and all your strength."

—Mark 12:30

GOD'S WORD FOR ME
BIBLE STORYBOOK

Illustrated by Marijke ten Cate

Compiled by Tama Fortner

Previously published as
The Begining Reader's Bible

A Division of Thomas Nelson Publishers

NASHVILLE   DALLAS   MEXICO CITY   RIO DE JANEIRO

ISBN 978-0-5291-0402-1

Printed in China
14 15 16 17 18 DSC 6 5 4 3 2 1

Mfr. R.R. Donnelley / Shenzhen, China / May 2014 / PO# 9290930

DEAR PARENTS,

There is nothing more precious than to see your children learn and grow in their knowledge of the Lord. *God's Word for Me Bible Storybook* was created to help them do just that.

Favorite stories from both the Old and New Testaments are presented using text from the *International Children's Bible®*. This translation was developed over many years by twenty-one scholars. It has been tested and has proven to be easy for children to read. So when your children read these stories, they aren't just reading an ordinary storybook. They are reading selected verses, in full or in part, of *actual Bible text*.

Memory verses, activities, and prayers accompany the stories to further reinforce your child's Bible experience—because the Bible isn't just about reading God's Word; it's about *living* God's Word.

At the end of the book, you'll find resources to help your children learn about the Bible and commit Scripture to memory. You'll also see a reading chart so that children can keep track of stories they have read—though they'll probably want to read them again and again!

THE PUBLISHER

Contents

Stories from the Old Testament

Stories from the New Testament

Resources to Guide Your Children

Stories from the
Old Testament

The Beginning of the World

Selections from Genesis 1 and 2

[1:1]In the beginning God created the sky and the earth. [3]Then God said, "Let there be light!" And there was light. [5]God named the light "day" and the darkness "night." This was the first day.

[7]God made the air to divide the water in two. Some of the water was above the air, and some of the water was below it. [8]God named the air "sky." This was the second day.

[9]Then God said, "Let the water under the sky be gathered together so the dry land will appear." [10]God named the dry land "earth." He named the water that was gathered together "seas." God saw that this was good.

[11]Then God said, "Let the earth produce plants. Every seed will produce more of its own kind of plant." [13]This was the third day.

[14]Then God said, "Let there be lights in the sky to separate day from night."

[16]So God made the two large lights. He made the brighter light to rule the day. He made the smaller light to rule the night. He also made the stars. [19]This was the fourth day.

Remember God's Word:
God looked at everything he had made, and it was very good.
—GENESIS 1:31

²⁰Then God said, "Let the water be filled with living things. And let birds fly in the air above the earth."

²¹So God created the large sea animals. He created every living thing that moves in the sea. God also made every bird that flies. God saw that this was good. ²²God blessed them and said, "Have many young ones and grow in number. Fill the water of the seas, and let the birds grow in number on the earth." ²³This was the fifth day.

Do God's Word:

Take a piece of paper and a pencil and go outside. Now take a look around. How many things can you see that God created? Grass and trees, flowers and birds, sunshine and rain. Draw a picture of something you're thankful God created.

[24]Then God said, "Let the earth be filled with animals. And let each produce more of its own kind. Let there be tame animals and small crawling animals and wild animals. And let each produce more of its kind." And it happened.

[25]God saw that this was good.

[27]God created human beings in his image. He created them male and female. [28]God blessed them and said, "Have many children and grow in number. Fill the earth and be its master. Rule over the fish in the sea and over the birds in the sky. Rule over every living thing that moves on the earth."

[31]God looked at everything he had made, and it was very good. This was the sixth day.

[2:1]So the sky, the earth and all that filled them were finished. [2]So on the seventh day he rested from all his work. [3]God blessed the seventh day and made it a holy day.

Pray God's Word:
I praise you because you made me
in an amazing and wonderful way.
What you have done is wonderful.
I know this very well.
—PSALM 139:14

The Very First Sin
Selections from Genesis 2 and 3

²:⁸The Lord God planted a garden called Eden. ⁹God caused every beautiful tree and every tree that was good for food to grow out of the ground. In the middle of the garden, God put the tree that gives life. And he put there the tree that gives the knowledge of good and evil.

¹⁵God put the man in the garden to care for it and work it. ¹⁶God commanded him, "You may eat the fruit from any tree in the garden. ¹⁷But you must not eat the fruit from the tree which gives the knowledge of good and evil. If you ever eat fruit from that tree, you will die!"

³:¹Now the snake was the most clever of all the wild animals God had made. One day the snake spoke to the woman. He said, "Did God really say that you must not eat fruit from any tree in the garden?"

²The woman answered, "We may eat fruit from the trees. ³But God told us, 'You must not eat fruit from the tree that is in the middle of the garden, or you will die.'"

⁴But the snake said to the woman, "You will not die. ⁵God knows that if you eat the fruit from that tree, you will learn about good and evil. Then you will be like God!"

⁶So she took some of its fruit and ate it. She also gave some of the fruit to her husband, and he ate it.

⁷Then, it was as if the man's and the woman's eyes were opened. They realized they were naked. So they made something to cover themselves.

Remember God's Word:
The Lord God put the man in the garden of Eden to care for it and work it.
—GENESIS 2:15

[8]Then they heard the Lord God walking in the garden. And the man and his wife hid. [9]God called to the man, "Where are you?"

[10]The man answered, "I heard you walking in the garden. I was afraid because I was naked. So I hid."

[11]God said to the man, "Who told you that you were naked? Did you eat fruit from that tree?"

[12]The man said, "You gave this woman to me. She gave me fruit from the tree. So I ate it."

[13]God said to the woman, "What have you done?"

She answered, "The snake tricked me. So I ate the fruit."

[14]God said to the snake, "A curse will be put on you. You will crawl on your stomach, and you will eat dust all the days of your life."

[17]God said to the man, "You ate fruit from the tree that I commanded you not to eat from. So I will put a curse on the ground. [18]The ground will produce thorns and weeds for you. [19]You will sweat and work hard for your food. And when you die, you will return to the dust."

[21]The Lord God made clothes from animal skins for the man and his wife. [22]Then God said, "The man knows good and evil. We must keep him from eating some of the fruit from the tree of life. If he does, he will live forever." [23]So the Lord God forced the man out of the garden of Eden.

Pray God's Word:
My king and my God, I pray to you.
Lord, every morning you hear my voice.
Every morning, I tell you what I need.
And I wait for your answer.
Show me the right thing to do.
Show me clearly how you want me to live.
—PSALM 5:2–3, 8

Do God's Word:

God still wants us to take care of his world. Go outside and look around. Do you see any trash lying on the ground? Pick it up and throw it in the garbage can. Or get a seed and plant a flower or a tree. Take care of your pets. Feed the birds. Learn how to recycle. There's so much you can do to take care of God's beautiful world!

Noah and the Great Flood

Selections from Genesis 6–9

6:9Noah was a good man. He walked with God. 10Noah had three sons: Shem, Ham and Japheth.

11People on earth did what God said was evil. 12And God saw this evil. All people on the earth did only evil. 13So God said to Noah, "People have made the earth full of violence. So I will destroy all people from the earth. 14Build a boat of cypress wood for yourself. Make rooms in it and cover it inside and outside with tar. 16Make an opening around the top of the boat. Put a door in the side of the boat. Make an upper, middle and lower deck in it. 17I will bring a flood of water on the earth. Everything on the earth will die. 18But I will make an agreement with you. You, your sons, your wife and your sons' wives will all go into the boat."

Pray God's Word:
Lord, keep us safe. Always protect us.
Protect me, God, because I trust in you.
　　—Psalm 12:7; 16:1

13

¹⁹"You must bring into the boat two of every living thing, male and female. Keep them alive with you. ²¹Also gather some of every kind of food. Store it on the boat as food for you and the animals."

²²Noah did everything that God commanded him.

^{7:1}Then the Lord said to Noah, ⁴"Seven days from now I will send rain on the earth. It will rain 40 days and 40 nights."

¹⁰Seven days later the flood started. ¹¹The underground springs split open. And the clouds in the sky poured out rain.

¹³On that same day Noah and his wife, his sons Shem, Ham and Japheth and their wives went into the boat. ¹⁴They had every kind of wild animal and tame animal. There was every kind of animal that crawls on the earth. Every kind of bird was there. ¹⁵They all came to Noah in the boat in groups of two. ¹⁶One male and one female of every living thing came. It was just as God had commanded Noah. Then the Lord closed the door behind them.

¹⁷Water flooded the earth for 40 days. As the water rose, it lifted the boat off the ground. ¹⁹The water rose so much that even the highest mountains were covered by it.

²¹All living things that moved on the earth died. ²³All that was left was Noah and

what was with him in the boat. [24]And the waters continued to cover the earth for 150 days. [8:1]But God remembered Noah and all the wild animals and tame animals with him in the boat. God made a wind blow over the earth. And the water went down. [2]The underground springs stopped flowing. And the clouds in the sky stopped pouring down rain.

[6]Forty days later Noah opened the window in the boat. [7]He sent out a raven. It flew here and there until the water had dried up from the earth. [8]Then Noah sent out a dove. [9]The dove could not find a place to land. So it came back to the boat.

[10]After seven days Noah again sent out the dove. [11]It came back with a fresh olive leaf in its mouth. Then Noah knew that the ground was almost dry. [12]Seven days later he sent the dove out again. But this time it did not come back.

[15]God said to Noah, [16]"Go out of the boat. [17]Bring every animal out of the boat with you."

[9:1]Then God blessed Noah and his sons. He said to them, "Have many children. Grow in number and fill the earth."

[8]Then God said, [11]"I will never again destroy all living things by floodwaters. [13]I am putting my rainbow in the clouds. [17]It is the sign of the agreement that I made with all living things on earth."

Remember God's Word:

"I am putting my rainbow in the clouds."
—GENESIS 9:13

Do God's Word:

Draw your own rainbow. Use all your favorite colors.
Remember that God *always* keeps his promises. And he wants
you to keep your promises too!

Remember God's Word:
Go and make followers of all people in the world.
—MATTHEW 28:19

20

A Tower Called "Babel"

Selections from Genesis 11

11:1At this time the whole world spoke one language. Everyone used the same words. 2As people moved from the East, they found a plain in the land of Babylonia. They settled there to live.

³They said to each other, "Let's make bricks and bake them to make them hard." So they used bricks instead of stones, and tar instead of mortar. ⁴Then they said to each other, "Let's build for ourselves a city and a tower. And let's make the top of the tower reach high into the sky. We will become famous. If we do this, we will not be scattered over all the earth."

Pray God's Word:
I will praise you more and more.
I will tell about how you do what is right.
I will tell about your salvation all day long.
—PSALM 71:14–15

[5]The Lord came down to see the city and the tower that the people had built. [6]The Lord said, "Now, these people are united. They all speak the same language. This is only the beginning of what they will do. They will be able to do anything they want. [7]Come, let us go down and confuse their language. Then they will not be able to understand each other."

⁸So the Lord scattered them from there over all the earth. And they stopped building the city. ⁹That is where the Lord confused the language of the whole world. So the place is called Babel. So the Lord caused them to spread out from there over all the whole world.

Do God's Word:

Today there are more than 6,000 different languages in the world! And God wants every person in the world—no matter what language they speak—to know that he loves them. Try learning some different ways to say, "God loves you."

English: God loves you.   French: Dieu t'aime.
Spanish: Dios te ama.   German: Gott liebt dich.
Italian: Dio ti ama.   Dutch: God houdt van je.

God Makes a Promise

Selections from Genesis 12, 15, 17, 18, and 21

12:1The Lord said to Abram, "Leave your country, your relatives and your father's family. Go to the land I will show you. 2I will make you a great nation, and I will bless you. I will make you famous. And you will be a blessing to others. 3I will bless those who bless you. I will place a curse on those who harm you. And all the people on earth will be blessed through you."

4So Abram left Haran as the Lord had told him. At this time Abram was 75 years old. 5Abram took his wife Sarai and everything they owned. They took all the servants they had gotten in Haran. They set out from Haran, planning to go to the land of Canaan. In time they arrived there.

¹⁵:¹After these things happened, the Lord spoke to Abram in a vision. God said, "Abram, don't be afraid. I will give you a great reward."

²But Abram said, "Lord God, what can you give me? I have no son."

⁴Then the Lord said, "You will have a son."

⁵Then God led Abram outside. God said, "Look at the sky. There are so many stars you cannot count them. And your descendants will be too many to count."

¹⁷:¹When Abram was 99 years old, the Lord said, ⁴"I will make you the father of many nations. ⁵I am changing your name from Abram to Abraham. ⁶I will give you many descendants. Kings will come from you. ⁷I will be your God and the God of all your descendants.

¹⁵"I will change the name of Sarai, your wife. Her new name will be Sarah. ¹⁶I will bless her. I will give her a son, and you will be the father. She will be the mother of many nations. Kings of nations will come from her."

Pray God's Word:
I look at the heavens,
which you made with your hands.
I see the moon and stars,
which you created.
Lord our Master,
your name is the most wonderful name in all the earth!
—PSALM 8:3, 9

18:1Later, the Lord again appeared to Abraham. Abraham was sitting at the door of his tent. 2He looked up and saw three men. Abraham bowed facedown on the ground before them. 3Abraham said, "Please stay awhile with me. 5I will get some bread for you, so you can regain your strength. Then you may continue your journey."

The three men said, "That is fine. Do as you said."

6Abraham hurried to Sarah. He said to her, "Hurry, prepare loaves of bread." 7Then Abraham took one of his best calves to a servant to prepare it for food. 8Abraham gave the three men the calf that had been cooked. While the three men ate, he stood under the tree near them.

9The men asked Abraham, "Where is your wife Sarah?"

"There, in the tent," said Abraham.

10Then the Lord said, "I will certainly return to you about this time a year from now. At that time your wife Sarah will have a son."

Sarah was listening at the entrance of the tent. 11Abraham and Sarah were very old.

12So she laughed to herself, "My husband and I are too old to have a baby."

13Then the Lord said to Abraham, "Why did Sarah laugh? 14Is anything too hard for the Lord? No! Sarah will have a son."

16Then the men got up to leave.

²¹:¹The Lord cared for Sarah as he had said. He did for her what he had promised. ²Sarah became pregnant. And she gave birth to a son for Abraham in his old age. Everything happened at the time God had said it would. ³Abraham named his son Isaac.

⁵Abraham was 100 years old when his son Isaac was born. ⁶And Sarah said, "God has made me laugh. Everyone who hears about this will laugh with me. ⁷No one thought that I would be able to have Abraham's child. But I have given Abraham a son while he is old."

Do God's Word:

Tonight, go outside with your family and look at the stars. How many do you think you can see? Ask your family if they know any of the stars' names. Maybe they will show you the Big Dipper, the North Star, or the Milky Way. Isn't the sky big and wide? As you are looking up at the night sky, remember that God's love for you is even bigger than that!

Remember God's Word:

Every good action and every perfect gift is from God.
—JAMES 1:17

Joseph and His Brothers

Selections from Genesis 37, 39, 41–43, and 45–46

[37:2]Joseph was a young man, 17 years old. [3]Joseph was born when his father, Jacob, was old. He made Joseph a special robe. [4]Joseph's brothers saw that their father loved Joseph more than he loved them. So they hated their brother.

[12]One day Joseph's brothers went to herd their father's sheep. [13]Jacob said to Joseph, [14]"Go and see if your brothers and the sheep are all right."

[18]Joseph's brothers saw him coming from far away. [19]They said, [20]"Let's kill him and throw his body into one of the wells."

[21]But Reuben said, "Let's not kill him. [22]Throw him into this well. But don't hurt him!" [23]So when Joseph came, they pulled off his robe. [24]Then they threw him into the well. There was no water in it.

[26]Judah said to his brothers, "What will we gain if we kill our brother? [27]Let's sell him." The other brothers agreed. [28]So when traders came by, the brothers sold him for eight ounces of silver.

[31]The brothers killed a goat and dipped Joseph's robe in its blood. [32]Then they brought the robe to their father.

[33]Jacob looked it over and said, "It is my son's robe! Some savage animal has eaten him." [34]Jacob continued to be sad about his son for a long time.

Pray God's Word:
May my friends sing and shout for joy.
May they always say, "Praise the greatness of the Lord. He loves to see his servants do well."
I will tell of your goodness.
I will praise you every day.
　　—PSALM 35:27–28

37

^{39:1}Joseph had been taken down to Egypt. An Egyptian named Potiphar bought Joseph. ³Potiphar saw that the Lord was with Joseph. ⁴He put Joseph in charge of the house.

⁶Now Joseph was handsome. ⁷After some time the wife of Joseph's master began to desire Joseph, ¹⁰but he refused to even spend time with her.

¹¹One day ¹²his master's wife grabbed his coat. She said, "Come with me." But Joseph left his coat in her hand and ran out of the house.

¹⁷She told her husband, "This Hebrew slave you brought here came in to shame me! ¹⁸When he came near me, I screamed. He ran away, but he left his coat." ²⁰So Potiphar arrested Joseph and put him into prison.

²¹But the Lord was with Joseph. The Lord caused the prison warden to like Joseph. ²²The warden chose Joseph to take care of all the prisoners. ²³The Lord made Joseph successful in everything he did.

[41:1]Two years later the king had a dream. [14]The king called for Joseph. [15]The king said, "I have had a dream. But no one can explain its meaning to me. I have heard that you can explain a dream."

[16]Joseph answered, "I am not able to explain dreams. God will do this for the king. [25]God is telling you what he is about to do. [29]You will have seven years of good crops in Egypt. [30]But after those seven years, there will come seven years of hunger.

[33]"So let the king choose a man who is very wise and set him over Egypt. [34]Take one-fifth of all the food that is grown during the seven good years. [36]That food will be used during the seven years of hunger. Then the people in Egypt will not die."

[39]So the king said to Joseph, [40]"I will put you in charge. All the people will obey your orders."

[46]Joseph was 30 years old when he began serving the king of Egypt. [48]Joseph gathered all the food produced during those seven years of good crops. In every city he stored grain. [49]He stored so much grain that he could not measure it.

[54]The seven years of hunger began, just as Joseph had said. In all the lands people had nothing to eat. But in Egypt there was food. [57]All the people in that part of the world came to Joseph to buy grain.

[42:3]Ten of Joseph's brothers went down to buy grain from Egypt. [6]Now Joseph was the one who sold the grain to people. So Joseph's brothers came to him.

[8]Joseph knew they were his brothers. But they did not know who he was. [9]He said to them, "You are spies!"

[10]But his brothers said, "No. We come just to buy food. [13]We are 10 of 12 brothers. Our youngest brother is with our father right now. And our other brother is gone."

[14]But Joseph said, "You are spies!" [17]Then Joseph put them all in prison for three days.

¹⁸On the third day Joseph said, ¹⁹"If you are honest men, let one of your brothers stay here in prison. The rest of you go and carry grain back to feed your hungry families. ²⁰Then bring your youngest brother back here to me. If you do this, I will know you are telling the truth."

The brothers agreed to this.

²⁹The brothers went to their father Jacob in Canaan. They told him everything that had happened. ³⁰They said, ³³"The master of the land said to us, ³⁴'Bring your youngest brother to me.'"

³⁸But Jacob said, "I will not allow Benjamin to go with you."

43:1Still no food grew in the land of Canaan. 2Jacob's family had eaten all the grain they had brought from Egypt. So Jacob said, "Go to Egypt again. Buy a little more grain for us to eat. 13Take Benjamin with you. 14I pray that God All-Powerful will cause the governor to be merciful to you."

15So the brothers hurried down to Egypt and stood before Joseph. 16Joseph said to the servant in charge of his house, "Bring those men into my house. Those men will eat with me today at noon."

18The brothers were afraid when they were brought to Joseph's house. 26The brothers bowed down to the ground to him.

30Joseph had to hold back the tears when he saw his brother Benjamin. 31He controlled himself and said, "Serve the meal."

32They served Joseph at one table. They served his brothers at another table. 33Joseph's brothers were seated in front of him. They were in order of their ages, from oldest to youngest. 34Food from Joseph's table was taken to them.

> ## Remember God's Word:
> Don't say, "I'll pay you back for the evil you did."
> Wait for the Lord. He will make things right.
> —Proverbs 20:22

[45:1]Joseph could not control himself any longer. He cried out, [4]"I am your brother Joseph. You sold me as a slave to go to Egypt. [5]Now don't be worried. [7]God sent me here ahead of you to keep you alive in an amazing way.

[9]"So go to my father. Tell him, 'Your son Joseph says: God has made me master over all Egypt. Come down to me quickly. [11]I will care for you during the years of hunger. In this way, you and your family will not starve.'"

[25]So the brothers went to Jacob. [26]They told him, "Joseph is still alive. He is the ruler over all Egypt."

[28]Jacob said, "I will go and see him."

[46:6]So Jacob went to Egypt. [7]He took all his family with him. [29]Joseph went to meet his father. As soon as Joseph saw his father, he hugged his neck. And he cried there for a long time.

Do God's Word:

Joseph could have been very mean to his brothers when they came to him for food. After all, they had been very mean to him. But Joseph *chose* to be kind to his brothers and to forgive them.

God wants you to choose to be kind also. When someone hurts your feelings, instead of saying something mean, try saying something nice about that person. Choosing to be kind makes God smile!

Moses and the Stubborn King

Selections from Exodus 1, 3, 5, and 7–14

1:8A new king began to rule Egypt. He did not know who Joseph was. 9This king said to his people, "Look! The people of Israel are too many!" 11So the Egyptians put slave masters over the Israelites.

3:1One day 2the angel of the Lord appeared to Moses in flames of fire coming out of a bush. Moses saw that the bush was on fire, but it was not burning up.

4God called to him from the bush, "Moses, Moses!"

And Moses said, "Here I am."

5Then God said, "Do not come any closer. Take off your sandals. You are standing on holy ground. 6I am the God of your ancestors. I am the God of Abraham, the God of Isaac and the God of Jacob." Moses covered his face because he was afraid to look at God.

7The Lord said, "I have seen the troubles my people have suffered in Egypt. And I have heard their cries when the Egyptian slave masters hurt them. 10So now I am sending you to the king of Egypt. Go! Bring my people, the Israelites, out of Egypt!"

Remember God's Word:
The Lord says,
"I will make you wise.
I will show you where to go.
I will guide you and watch over you."
—PSALM 32:8

5:1Moses went to the king of Egypt. "This is what the Lord, the God of Israel says: 'Let my people go.'"

2But the king of Egypt said, "Who is the Lord? Why should I obey him? I will not let Israel go."

7:14Then the Lord said to Moses, "The king is being stubborn. 15In the morning the king will go out to the Nile River. Go meet him by the edge of the river. Take with you the walking stick. 16Tell him this: 17"This is how you will know that I am the Lord. I will strike the water of the Nile River with this stick. And the water will change into blood.'"

20So Moses did just as the Lord had commanded. All the water in the Nile changed into blood. 21The fish in the Nile died, and the river began to stink. So the Egyptians could not drink water from it.

23The king ignored what Moses had done. 25Seven days passed.

8:6Frogs came up out of the water and covered the land. 17Then the dust changed into gnats. The gnats got on the people. 19But the king was stubborn and refused to listen.

24Great swarms of flies came.
9:6All the farm animals died. 7But the king did not let the people go.

10Moses threw ashes into the air. It caused boils to break out and become sores on people and animals. 25Hail destroyed everything that grew in the fields. 35The king refused to let the Israelites go.
10:14Swarms of locusts 15ate everything. 22Then total darkness was everywhere in Egypt for three days. 27But the king refused to let them go.
11:1The Lord told Moses, "I have one more way to punish the king. After this, he will force you to leave."
12:29The Lord killed all the firstborn sons in the land of Egypt. The firstborn of the king, who sat on the throne, died. Even the firstborn of the prisoner in jail died. 30Someone died in every house. So there was loud crying everywhere in Egypt.

Pray God's Word:
I praise the Lord because he guides me.
Even at night, I feel his leading.
—PSALM 16:7

53

³¹During the night the king
called for Moses. He said, "Leave."
¹³:¹⁷The king sent the people out of Egypt. ¹⁸God led them
through the desert toward the Red Sea.
¹⁴:⁵The king of Egypt was told that the people of Israel had left. Then he and his
officers changed their minds about them. They said, "What have we
done? We have lost our slaves!" ⁶So the king ⁷took 600 of his best chariots.
⁹And they chased the Israelites.

¹⁰The Israelites were very frightened and cried to the Lord for help.

¹³But Moses answered, "Don't be afraid! ¹⁴The Lord will fight for you."

¹⁵Then the Lord said to Moses, ¹⁶"Raise your walking stick and hold it over the sea."

²¹Moses held his hand over the sea. All that night the Lord drove back the sea with a strong east
wind. ²²And the Israelites went through the sea on dry land. A wall of water was on both sides.
²³Then all the king's horses, chariots and chariot drivers followed them into the sea.

²⁶The Lord told Moses, "Hold your hand over the sea." ²⁷So Moses raised his hand over the sea.
The water became deep again. The Egyptians were swept away into the sea.

³⁰So that day the Lord saved the Israelites from the Egyptians.

Do God's Word:

Maps are wonderful things. They show you just how to get where you want to go. Did you know that the Bible is a map?

It is a map to heaven. When you read and follow God's Word, it will show you just how to get to heaven. Try to read from God's Word every day.

Rahab and the Spies

Selections from Joshua 1, 2, and 6

1:1Joshua was Moses' assistant. After Moses died, the Lord said to Joshua: 2"You and all these people go across the Jordan River. 3I promised Moses I would give you this land. 5Just as I was with Moses, so I will be with you.

6"Be strong and brave! You must lead these people so they can take their land. 9Don't be afraid. The Lord your God will be with you everywhere you go."

2:1Joshua secretly sent out two spies. Joshua said to them, "Go and look closely at the city of Jericho."

So the men went to Jericho to the house of Rahab.

2Someone told the king of Jericho, "Some men from Israel have come here tonight. They are spying out the land."

3So the king of Jericho sent this message to Rahab: "Bring out the men who entered your house. They have come to spy out our whole land."

4Now the woman had hidden the two men. She said, "They did come here. But I didn't know where they came from. 5In the evening, they left. I don't know where they went. Go quickly. Maybe you can catch them." 6(But the woman had taken the men up to the roof. She had hidden them there under stalks of flax.) 7So the king's men went out looking for the spies.

> ## Remember God's Word:
> The Lord your God will be with you everywhere you go.
> —JOSHUA 1:9

Pray God's Word:
I go to bed and sleep in peace.
Lord, only you keep me safe.
Protect me, because I worship you.

—Psalm 4:8; 86:2

⁸The spies were ready to sleep for the night. So Rahab went to the roof and ⁹said, "I know the Lord has given this land to your people. ¹²So now, make me a promise before the Lord. ¹³Promise me you will allow my family to live."

¹⁴The men agreed. They said, "When the Lord gives us our land, we will be kind to you."

¹⁵The house Rahab lived in was built on the city wall. So she used a rope to let the men down through a window. ¹⁶She said to them, "Go into the hills. The king's men will not find you there."

¹⁷The men said to her, ¹⁸"You are using a red rope to help us escape. When we return, you must tie it in the window. Bring all your family into your house. ¹⁹We can keep everyone safe who stays in this house."

²¹Rahab answered, "I agree to this." So she sent them away. Then she tied the red rope in the window.

²²The men left and went into the hills. The king's men returned to the city without finding them. ²³Then the two men went to Joshua and told him everything.

⁶:²Then the Lord spoke to Joshua. He said, "Look, I have given you Jericho. ³March around the city with your army one time every day. Do this for six days. ⁴On the seventh day march around the city seven times. On that day tell the priests to blow the trumpets as they march. ⁵They will make one long blast on the trumpets. When you hear that sound, have all the people give a loud shout. Then the walls of the city will fall. And the people will go straight into the city."

⁷Then Joshua ordered the people, "Now go! March around the city." ¹⁴They did this every day for six days.

¹⁵On the seventh day they marched around the city seven times. ¹⁶The seventh time around the priests blew their trumpets. Then Joshua gave the command: "Now, shout! The Lord has given you this city!"

²⁰The people shouted. The walls fell. The Israelites defeated that city.

²⁵Joshua saved Rahab, her family and all who were with her. This was because Rahab had helped the men he had sent to spy out Jericho.

61

The Story of Ruth

Selections from the Book of Ruth

1:1-2Long ago, there was a time when there was not enough food to eat. A man named Elimelech left Bethlehem and moved to the country of Moab. He took his wife and his two sons with him. His wife was named Naomi, and his two sons were named Mahlon and Kilion. 3Later, Naomi's husband died. So only Naomi and her two sons were left. 4These sons married women from Moab. One was Orpah. The other was Ruth. 5Then Mahlon and Kilion also died.

6Naomi got ready to go back home. 8Naomi said to her two daughters-in-law, "Each of you go to your own mother's house. 9I hope the Lord will give you another home and a new husband."

14Orpah kissed Naomi good-bye, but Ruth held on to her.

16Ruth said, "Don't ask me to leave you! Every place you go, I will go. Your people will be my people. Your God will be my God."

18Naomi saw that Ruth had made up her mind to go with her. So 19Naomi and Ruth went on until they came to the town of Bethlehem.

Remember God's Word:
Then the King will answer, "I tell you the truth. Anything you did for any of my people here, you also did for me."
—MATTHEW 25:40

²:¹Now there was a rich man living in Bethlehem whose name was Boaz. Boaz was one of Naomi's close relatives.

²One day Ruth said to Naomi, "Let me go to the fields. Maybe someone will be kind and let me gather the grain he leaves in his field."

³So Ruth went to the fields. She followed the workers and she gathered the grain that they had left. It just so happened that the field belonged to Boaz.

⁵Boaz spoke to his servant. He asked, "Whose girl is that?"

⁶The servant answered, "She is the Moabite woman who came with Naomi. ⁷She said, 'Please let me follow the workers and gather the grain that they leave on the ground.' From morning until just now, she has stopped only a few moments to rest."

⁸Then Boaz said to Ruth, "Listen, my daughter. Stay here in my field to gather grain. ⁹When you are thirsty, take water from the jugs the servants have filled."

¹⁰Then Ruth bowed low. She said to Boaz, "I am a stranger. Why have you been so kind to notice me?"

¹¹Boaz answered her, "I know about all the help you have given to Naomi. ¹²The Lord will reward you for all you have done."

¹⁵Then Boaz told his servants, ¹⁶"Drop some full heads of grain for her. Let her gather that grain, and don't tell her to stop."

¹⁷So Ruth gathered grain in the field until evening. Then she separated the grain from the chaff. There was about one-half bushel of barley.

¹⁹Naomi asked her, "Where did you gather all this grain today?"
Ruth said, "The man I worked with today is named Boaz."

²⁰Naomi told her daughter-in-law, "The Lord bless him! Boaz is one of our close relatives, one who will take care of us."

Do God's Word:

Think of some ways that you can be a friend to your elderly neighbor who can't quite make it to the mailbox anymore, to the boy who's always the last one picked for the dodgeball team, or to the little girl who eats lunch by herself every day.

Think about a way that you can be a friend to someone in your own home. Remember, when you are being a friend to someone in need, you are also being a friend to Jesus (Matthew 25:40).

Hannah's Special Baby

Selections from 1 Samuel 1–3

[1:1]There was a man named Elkanah. [2]Elkanah had two wives. One was named Hannah, and the other was named Peninnah. Peninnah had children, but Hannah had none.

[3]Every year Elkanah went up to Shiloh. There he worshiped the Lord and offered sacrifices to him. [9]Once, after they had eaten their meal in Shiloh, Hannah got up. Now Eli the priest was sitting near the Lord's Holy Tent. [10]Hannah cried much and prayed to the Lord. [11]She said, "Lord, remember me! If you will give me a son, I will give him back to you all his life."

[12]While Hannah kept praying, Eli watched her. [14]He said to her, [17]"May God give you what you asked of him." [18]Hannah left and was not sad anymore.

[19]The Lord remembered, [20]and in time she gave birth to a son. She named him Samuel.

> **Remember God's Word**
> I will pray to the Lord.
> And he will answer me.
> —PSALM 3:4

[21] Every year Elkanah went to Shiloh to offer sacrifices. He brought his whole family with him. [22] But Hannah did not go. She told him, "When the boy is old enough to eat solid food, I will take him to Shiloh. Then I will give him to the Lord." [23] Elkanah said to her, "Do what you think is best."

[24] When Samuel was old enough, Hannah took him to the Tent of the Lord at Shiloh. [26] She said to Eli, [27] "I prayed for this child. The Lord answered my prayer and gave him to me. [28] Now I give him back to the Lord. He will belong to the Lord all his life."

[2:19] Every year Samuel's mother would make a little coat for him. She would take it to him when she went to Shiloh.

[21] The Lord was kind to Hannah. She became the mother of three sons and two daughters. The boy Samuel grew up serving the Lord.

Pray God's Word:
Lord, you are a God who shows mercy and is kind.
Show me a sign of your goodness.
When I cry for help, answer me quickly.
My God, you are very great.
—PSALM 86:15, 17; 102:2; 104:1

[26]He pleased God and the people.

[3:2]One night [4]the Lord called Samuel. Samuel answered, "I am here!" [5]He ran to Eli and said, "I am here. You called me."

But Eli said, "I didn't call you. Go back to bed." So Samuel went back to bed.

[6]The Lord called again, "Samuel!"

Samuel again went to Eli. Again Eli said, "I didn't call you. Go back to bed."

[8]The Lord called Samuel for the third time. Samuel went to Eli. He said, "I am here. You called me."

Then Eli realized the Lord was calling the boy. [9]So he told Samuel, "Go to bed. If he calls you again, say, 'Speak, Lord. I am your servant, and I am listening.'" So Samuel went and lay down in bed.

[10]The Lord called as he had before. He said, "Samuel, Samuel!"

Samuel said, "Speak, Lord. I am your servant, and I am listening."

[19]The Lord was with Samuel as he grew up. [20]All Israel knew Samuel was a prophet of the Lord.

Do God's Word:

God loves to hear from you. And he hears every single prayer you say. And God always answers—but sometimes he answers in ways you might not expect!

To help you see how powerful prayers are, make a Prayer Poster. Jot down all the things you pray for. Then watch and see how God works through your prayers!

David and the Great Big Giant

Selections from 1 Samuel 17

17:1The Philistines gathered their armies for war. 3The Philistines controlled one hill. The Israelites controlled another. The valley was between them.

4The Philistines had a champion fighter named Goliath. He was about nine feet four inches tall. 8Goliath shouted to the Israelite soldiers, "Choose a man to fight me. 9If he can kill me, we will become your servants. But if I kill him, you will become our servants." 11Saul and the Israelites were very afraid.

12Now David was the son of Jesse. Jesse was from Bethlehem. 13His three oldest sons followed Saul to the war. 14David was the youngest son. 15David took care of his father's sheep.

17Jesse said to David, 18"See how your brothers are. 19They are fighting against the Philistines."

20When David arrived at the camp, 21the Israelites and Philistines were lining up their men to face each other in battle. 23Goliath came out. He shouted things against Israel as usual, and David heard it.

> ### Pray God's Word:
> Lord my God, help me.
> Because you are loving, save me.
> —PSALM 109:26

³²David said to Saul, "I will go and fight this Philistine!"

³³Saul answered, "You can't go out against this Philistine and fight him. You're only a boy."

³⁴But David said to Saul, "I, your servant, have been keeping my father's sheep. When a lion or bear came and took a sheep from the flock, ³⁵I would chase it. ³⁶I have killed both a lion and a bear! Goliath, the Philistine, will be like the lion or bear I killed. He will die because he has stood against the armies of the living God. ³⁷The Lord saved me from a lion and a bear. He will also save me from this Philistine."

Saul said to David, "Go, and may the Lord be with you."

Do God's Word:

What "giants" do you have in your life?

Go outside and find five smooth stones. Then think of one of your "giants." Maybe it's a bully at school. Whatever that giant is, God already knows about it, and he can fix the situation. Pray and ask him for help as you toss away the stones.

³⁹Then David ⁴⁰took his stick in his hand. And he chose five smooth stones from a stream. He put them in his pouch and held his sling in his hand. Then he went to meet Goliath.

⁴²Goliath looked down at David with disgust. ⁴³He said, "Do you think I am a dog, that you come at me with a stick? ⁴⁴Come here. I'll feed your body to the birds and the wild animals!"

⁴⁵But David said to him, "You come to me using a sword. But I come to you in the name of the Lord. You have spoken out against him. ⁴⁶Today the Lord will give you to me. ⁴⁷The battle belongs to him! And he will help us defeat all of you."

⁴⁸As Goliath came near to attack him, David ran quickly to meet him. ⁴⁹He took a stone from his pouch. He put it into his sling and slung it. The stone hit the Philistine on his forehead. Goliath fell facedown on the ground.

⁵⁰So David defeated the Philistine with only a sling and a stone! He hit him and killed him. ⁵¹When the Philistines saw that their champion was dead, they turned and ran.

Remember God's Word:
David defeated the Philistine with only a sling and a stone!
—1 Samuel 17:50

Nehemiah and the Broken-Down Wall

Selections from Nehemiah 1, 2, 4, 7, and 8

1:1I, Nehemiah, was in the capital city of Susa. 2One of my brothers came from Judah. Some other men were with him. I asked them about Jerusalem.

3They answered, "Nehemiah, the wall around Jerusalem is broken down. And its gates have been burned."

4When I heard these things, I sat down and cried for several days. I prayed. 5I said, 11"Lord, listen carefully to my prayer. Give me success today. Allow this king to show kindness to me."

I was the one who served wine to the king.

> ### Remember God's Word:
> First I prayed to the God of heaven.
> —NEHEMIAH 2:4

2:1King Artaxerxes was king. He wanted some wine. So I took some and gave it to the king. I had not been sad in his presence before. 2So the king said, "Why does your face look sad? You are not sick. Your heart must be sad."

3I said to the king, "My face is sad because the city where my ancestors are buried lies in ruins. And its gates have been destroyed by fire."

4Then the king said to me, "What do you want?"

First I prayed to the God of heaven. 5Then I answered the king, "Send me to the city in Judah where my ancestors are buried. I will rebuild it. Do this if you are willing and if I have pleased you."

6It pleased the king to send me.

[11]I went to Jerusalem. [13]I was inspecting the walls. They had been broken down. And the gates had been destroyed by fire. [16]I had not yet said anything to the Jews, the priests, the important men or the officers. I had not said anything to any of the others who would do the work.

[17]Then I said to them, "Jerusalem is a pile of ruins. And its gates have been burned. Come, let's rebuild the wall of Jerusalem. Then we won't be full of shame any longer."

[18]They answered, "Let's start rebuilding." So they began to work hard. [4:6]So we rebuilt the wall until all of it went halfway up. The people were willing to work hard.

[11]Our enemies said, "We will come among them and kill them. We will stop the work."

[16]From that day on, half my men worked on the wall. The other half was ready with spears, shields, bows and armor. [17]Those who carried materials did their work with one hand. They carried a weapon in the other hand. [18]Each builder wore his sword at his side as he worked. [23]Each person carried his weapon even when he went for water.

Do God's Word:

The wall of Jerusalem surrounded and protected God's people. Prayer does the same thing. When you talk to God, you are surrounded and protected.

Ask your parents if you can build a fort out of pillows and cushions. When you're done, hide in the middle and thank God for his protection.

Pray God's Word:

Do good to me, your servant, so I can live,
so I can obey your word.
Open my eyes to see the wonderful
things in your teachings.

—PSALM 119:17–18

^{7:1}After the wall had been rebuilt, ^{8:1}all the people of Israel gathered together. They asked Ezra the teacher to bring out the Book of the Teachings of Moses. ³Ezra read the Teachings out loud. He read from early morning until noon. All the people listened carefully.

¹⁰Nehemiah said, "Go and enjoy good food and sweet drinks. Today is a holy day to the Lord. Don't be sad. The joy of the Lord will make you strong."

¹²Then all the people celebrated with great joy.

Selections from Daniel 5 and 6

5:31A man named Darius became king.

6:1Darius thought it would be a good idea to choose 120 governors. They would rule through all of his kingdom. 3Daniel showed that he could do the work better than the other governors. Because of this, the king planned to put Daniel in charge of the whole kingdom. 4So the other governors tried to find reasons to accuse Daniel. But they could not find anything wrong with him. Daniel was trustworthy. He was not lazy and did not cheat the king. 5Finally these men said, "We must find something to complain about. It will have to be about his God."

6So the governors went as a group to the king. They said: "King Darius! 7We think the king should make this law: No one should pray to any god or man except to you for the next 30 days. Anyone who doesn't obey will be thrown into the lions' den. 8Now, our king, make the law. Write it down so it cannot be changed." 9So King Darius made the law and had it written.

¹⁰When Daniel heard that the new law had been written, he went to his house. He went to his upstairs room. Three times each day Daniel got down on his knees and prayed, just as he always had done.

¹¹Then those men went as a group and found Daniel. They saw him praying. ¹²So they went to the king. They said, "Didn't you write a law that says no one may pray to any god or man except you, our king? Doesn't it say that anyone who disobeys will be thrown into the lions' den?"

The king answered, "Yes, I wrote that law."

¹³Then those men said, "Daniel still prays to his God three times every day." ¹⁴The king became very upset. He decided he had to save Daniel. He worked until sunset trying to think of a way to save him.

¹⁵Then those men went as a group to the king. They said, "Remember, our king, no law or command given by the king can be changed."

Remember God's Word:
The Lord is my light and the one who saves me.
—PSALM 27:1

[16]So King Darius gave the order. They brought Daniel and threw him into the lions' den. The king said, "May the God you serve save you!" [17]A big stone was put over the opening of the lions' den. [18]Then King Darius went back to his palace. He did not eat that night. And he could not sleep.

[19]The next morning King Darius hurried to the lions' den. [20]He called out to Daniel. He said, "Daniel, has your God been able to save you from the lions?"

[21]Daniel answered, "My king, live forever! [22]My God sent his angel to close the lions' mouths. They have not hurt me."

[23]King Darius was very happy. He told his servants to lift Daniel out of the lions' den. [24]Then the king gave a command. The men who had accused Daniel were brought to the lions' den and thrown into it.

[25]Then King Darius wrote a letter. It was to all people and all nations:

[26]I am making a new law. This law is for people in every part of my kingdom. All of you must fear and respect the God of Daniel. Daniel's God is the living God.

Do God's Word:
Daniel chose to stand up for God. You can stand up for God too! Ask your parents to take you to the zoo. Make sure you go see the lions. Aren't they scary? Yet God saved Daniel from big, ferocious lions. You can count on him to take care of you too.

Pray God's Word:
Lord, I trust in you.
Listen to me.
Be my rock of protection.
—PSALM 31:1–2

Stories from the New Testament

Jesus Is Born!

Selections from Luke 1 and 2

[1:26–27]God sent the angel Gabriel to a virgin who lived in Nazareth, a town in Galilee. She was engaged to marry a man named Joseph. Her name was Mary. [28]The angel came to her and said, "Greetings! The Lord has blessed you and is with you."

[30]The angel said to her, "Don't be afraid, Mary, because God is pleased with you. [31]You will give birth to a son, and you will name him Jesus. [32]He will be great, and people will call him the Son of the Most High."

[34]Mary said to the angel, "How will this happen? I am a virgin!"

[35]The angel said to Mary, "The Holy Spirit will come upon you, and the power of the Most High will cover you. The baby will be holy. He will be called the Son of God."

[38]Mary said, "I am the servant girl of the Lord. Let this happen to me as you say!" Then the angel went away.

²:¹At that time, Augustus Caesar sent an order to all people. The order said that they must list their names in a register. ³And everyone went to their own towns to be registered.

⁴So Joseph left Nazareth. He went to the town of Bethlehem in Judea. This town was known as the town of David. Joseph went there because he was from the family of David. ⁵Joseph registered with Mary. (Mary was now pregnant.) ⁶While Joseph and Mary were in Bethlehem, the time came for her to have the baby. ⁷She gave birth to her first son. There were no rooms left in the inn. So she wrapped the baby with cloths and laid him in a box where animals are fed.

Remember
God's Word:
Today your Savior was
born in David's town.
He is Christ, the Lord.
—LUKE 2:11

[8]That night, some shepherds were in the fields nearby watching their sheep. [9]An angel of the Lord stood before them. Suddenly they became very frightened. [10]The angel said to them, "Don't be afraid, because I am bringing you some good news. It will be a joy to all the people. [11]Today your Savior was born in David's town. He is Christ, the Lord. [12]This is how you will know him: You will find a baby wrapped in cloths and lying in a feeding box."

[13]Then a very large group of angels from heaven joined the first angel. All the angels were praising God.

[16]So the shepherds went quickly and found Mary and Joseph. [17]They told what the angels had said about this child. [18]Everyone was amazed when they heard what the shepherds said to them. [20]Then the shepherds went back to their sheep, praising God and thanking him for everything that they had seen and heard. It was just as the angel had told them.

Do God's Word:

People usually celebrate the birth of Jesus at Christmastime. But Jesus' birth is a wonderful thing to celebrate anytime!

Invite a friend who may not know Jesus to church and tell that person all about the Savior. Because sharing Jesus is the best celebration of all!

[21]When the baby was eight days old, he was named Jesus.

[22]The time came for Mary and Joseph to do what the law of Moses taught. They took Jesus to Jerusalem to present him to the Lord.

[25]A man named Simeon lived in Jerusalem. He was a good man and very religious. [26]The Holy Spirit told Simeon that he would not die before he saw the Christ promised by the Lord. [27]The Spirit led Simeon to the Temple. Mary and Joseph brought the baby Jesus to the Temple. [28]Then Simeon took the baby in his arms and thanked God:

[29]"Now, Lord, you can let me die in peace. [30]I have seen your Salvation with my own eyes."

[33]Jesus' father and mother were amazed at what Simeon had said about him.

[39]Joseph and Mary finished doing everything that the law of the Lord commanded. Then they went home to Nazareth, their own town in Galilee. [40]The little child began to grow up. He became stronger and wiser, and God's blessings were with him.

Pray God's Word:
Lord, teach me your demands.
Then I will obey them until the end.
Help me understand, so I can obey your teachings.
I will obey them with all my heart.

—PSALM 119:33–34

The Boy Jesus in the Temple

Selections from Luke 2

2:41Every year Jesus' parents went to Jerusalem for the Passover Feast. 42When Jesus was 12 years old, they went to the feast as they always did. 43When the feast days were over, they went home. The boy Jesus stayed behind in Jerusalem, but his parents did not know it. 44Joseph and Mary traveled for a whole day. They thought that Jesus was with them in the group. Then they began to look for him among their family and friends, 45but they did not find him. So they went back to Jerusalem to look for him there.

> **Remember God's Word:**
> Jesus continued to learn more and more and to grow physically. People liked him, and he pleased God.
> —LUKE 2:52

⁴⁶After three days they found him. Jesus was sitting in the Temple with the religious teachers, listening to them and asking them questions. ⁴⁷All who heard him were amazed at his understanding and wise answers. ⁴⁸When Jesus' parents saw him, they were amazed. His mother said to him, "Son, why did you do this to us? Your father and I were very worried about you. We have been looking for you."

⁴⁹Jesus asked, "Why did you have to look for me? You should have known that I must be where my Father's work is!" ⁵⁰But they did not understand the meaning of what he said.

⁵¹Jesus went with them to Nazareth and obeyed them. His mother was still thinking about all that had happened. ⁵²Jesus continued to learn more and more and to grow physically. People liked him, and he pleased God.

Do God's Word:

Even Jesus studied God's Word! To help you study God's Word, make a bookmark for your Bible. Draw a picture of Jesus studying in the Temple on a small piece of poster board. Punch a hole in the top and add a ribbon, if you like. Then put it in your Bible to mark your place.

Make an extra one or two to share with Mom, Dad, your grandparents, or a friend. Encourage them to study God's Word too!

Pray God's Word:

You made me and formed me with your hands.
Give me understanding so I can learn your commands.
—PSALM 119:73

Jesus Teaches the People

Selections from Matthew 4–7

[4:23]Jesus went everywhere in Galilee. He taught in the synagogues and preached the Good News about the kingdom of heaven. And he healed all the people's diseases and sicknesses. [24]The news about Jesus spread. [25]Many people followed him.

[5:1]Jesus saw the crowds. He went up on a hill and sat down. His followers came to him. [2]Jesus taught the people and said:

[43]"You have heard that it was said, 'Love your neighbor and hate your enemies.' [44]But I tell you, love your enemies. Pray for those who hurt you.

[6:1]"When you do good things, don't do them in front of people to be seen by them. [3]When you give to the poor, give very secretly. Don't let anyone know what you are doing. [4]Your Father can see what is done in secret, and he will reward you."

Remember God's Word:
But I tell you, love your enemies.
Pray for those who hurt you.
—MATTHEW 5:44

[5]"When you pray, don't be like the hypocrites. They love to stand in the synagogues and on the street corners and pray loudly. They want people to see them pray. [6]When you pray, you should go into your room and close the door. Then pray to your Father who cannot be seen. Your Father can see what is done in secret, and he will reward you.

[14]"If you forgive others for the things they do wrong, then your Father in heaven will also forgive you for the things you do wrong. [15]But if you don't forgive the wrongs of others, then your Father in heaven will not forgive the wrong things you do.

[25]"Don't worry about the food you need to live. [26]Look at the birds in the air. They don't plant or harvest. But your heavenly Father feeds the birds. And you know that you are worth much more than the birds.

[7:12]"Do for other people the same things you want them to do for you."

[28]When Jesus finished saying these things, the people were amazed at his teaching.

Do God's Word:

Jesus wants us to love everyone, even those who are not nice to us.

Think about people who aren't nice to you, and pray for them. Tell God that you forgive them, and ask him to help them be nicer. Then ask God to help you be nice to them.

Pray God's Word:

"Our Father in heaven,
Forgive the sins we have done,
just as we have forgiven those
who did wrong to us."
—MATTHEW 6:9, 12

Zacchaeus, the Wee Little Man

Selections from Luke 19

19:1Jesus was going through the city of Jericho. 2In Jericho there was a man named Zacchaeus. He was a wealthy, very important tax collector. 3He wanted to see who Jesus was, but he was too short to see above the crowd. 4He ran ahead to a place where he knew Jesus would come. He climbed a sycamore tree so he could see Jesus.

> **Remember God's Word:**
> The Son of Man came to find lost people and save them.
> —LUKE 19:10

⁵When Jesus came to that place, he looked up and saw Zacchaeus in the tree. He said to him, "Zacchaeus, hurry and come down! I must stay at your house today."

⁶Zacchaeus came down quickly. He was pleased to have Jesus in his house. ⁷All the people saw this and began to complain, "Look at the kind of man Jesus stays with. Zacchaeus is a sinner!"

⁸But Zacchaeus said to the Lord, "I will give half of my money to the poor. If I have cheated anyone, I will pay that person back four times more!"

⁹Jesus said, "Salvation has come to this house today. This man truly belongs to the family of Abraham. ¹⁰The Son of Man came to find lost people and save them."

Do God's Word:
Sing this song about Zacchaeus:

Zacchaeus was a wee little man,
And a wee little man was he.
He climbed up in a sycamore tree,
For the Lord he wanted to see.
And as the Savior passed that way,
He looked up in that tree.
And he said, "Zacchaeus, you come down!
For I'm going to your house today.
For I'm going to your house to stay."

Pray God's Word:
Praise the Lord.
He alone is great.
He is greater than heaven and earth.
Lord, accept my willing praise.
And teach me your laws.
—Psalm 148:13; 119:108

Two Miracles

Selections from Luke 8

8:41A man named Jairus came to Jesus. Jairus was a ruler of the synagogue. He bowed down at Jesus' feet and begged him to come to his house. 42Jairus had only one daughter. She was 12 years old, and she was dying.

While Jesus was on his way to Jairus' house, the people were crowding all around him. 43A woman was there who had been bleeding for 12 years. No doctor was able to heal her. 44The woman came up behind Jesus and touched the edge of his coat. At that moment, her bleeding stopped. 45Then Jesus said, "Who touched me?"

> **Remember God's Word:**
> Don't be afraid; only believe.
> —MARK 5:36

Peter said, "Master, the people are all around you and are pushing against you."

[46]But Jesus said, "Someone did touch me! I felt power go out from me." [47]When the woman saw that she could not hide, she came forward, shaking. She bowed down before Jesus. While all the people listened, she told why she had touched him. Then, she said, she was healed immediately. [48]Jesus said to her, "Dear woman, you are healed because you believed. Go in peace."

⁴⁹While Jesus was still speaking, someone came from the house of the synagogue ruler and said to the ruler, "Your daughter has died! Don't bother the teacher now."

⁵⁰When Jesus heard this, he said to Jairus, "Don't be afraid. Just believe, and your daughter will be well."

Pray God's Word:
I do believe! Help me to believe more!

—MARK 9:24

[51]Jesus went to the house. He let only Peter, John, James, and the girl's father and mother go inside with him. [52]All the people were crying and feeling sad because the girl was dead. But Jesus said, "Don't cry. She is not dead; she is only sleeping."

[53]The people laughed at Jesus because they knew that the girl was dead. [54]But Jesus took her by the hand and called to her, "My child, stand up!" [55]Her spirit came back into her, and she stood up immediately. Jesus said, "Give her something to eat." [56]The girl's parents were amazed.

Do God's Word:

You can believe in God, and you can believe in God's Word. Every single word of the Bible is true. "The Lord's teachings are perfect. They are worth more than gold, even the purest gold" (Psalm 19:7, 10).

Have a treasure hunt with God's Word. Write down some favorite verses on round pieces of gold paper (or have someone help you). Have someone hide these "gold coins" around the house or yard. Then see how quickly you can find them!

A Miracle for Dinner

Selections from Mark 6

^{6:30}The apostles that Jesus had sent out to preach returned. They gathered around him and told him about all the things they had done and taught. ³¹Crowds of people were coming and going. Jesus and his followers did not even have time to eat. He said to them, "Come with me. We will go to a quiet place. There we will get some rest."

³²So they went in a boat alone to a place where there were no people. ³³But many people saw them leave. So people from all the towns ran to where Jesus was going. They got there before Jesus arrived. ³⁴When he landed, he saw a great crowd waiting. Jesus felt sorry for them, because they were like sheep without a shepherd. So he taught them many things.

> **Remember God's Word:**
> Jesus looked up to heaven and thanked God for the bread.
> —MARK 6:41

³⁵It was now late in the day. Jesus' followers came to him and said, "It is already very late. ³⁶Send the people away. They need to go buy some food to eat."

³⁷But Jesus answered, "You give them food to eat."

They said to him, "We can't buy enough bread to feed all these people! We would all have to work a month to earn enough money to buy that much bread!"

³⁸Jesus asked them, "How many loaves of bread do you have now? Go and see."

When they found out, they came to him and said, "We have five loaves and two fish."

[39]Then Jesus said to the followers, "Tell all the people to sit in groups on the green grass." [40]So all the people sat in groups. They sat in groups of 50 or groups of 100. [41]Jesus took the five loaves and two fish. He looked up to heaven and thanked God for the bread. He divided the bread and gave it to his followers for them to give to the people. Then he divided the two fish among them all. [42]All the people ate and were satisfied. [43]The followers filled 12 baskets with the pieces of bread and fish that were not eaten. [44]There were about 5,000 men there who ate.

Do God's Word:

It's baking day! With a parent, bake a loaf of fresh, homemade bread. Be patient. It takes a while to make bread with yeast.

When your bread has baked, serve it to your friends or your family. But before you eat, remember—Jesus thanked God for the bread. Be just like Jesus, and thank God for your food too.

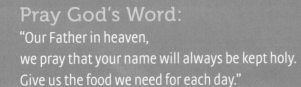

Pray God's Word:
"Our Father in heaven,
we pray that your name will always be kept holy.
Give us the food we need for each day."
—MATTHEW 6:9, 11

Remember God's Word:
Come back to God, and he will forgive your sins.
—ACTS 3:19

A Runaway Boy Comes Home

Selections from Luke 15

15:11Jesus said, "A man had two sons. 12The younger son said to his father, 'Give me my share of the property.' So the father divided the property between his two sons. 13Then the younger son gathered up all that was his and left. He traveled far away to another country.

"There he wasted his money in foolish living. [14]He spent everything that he had. Soon after that, the land became very dry, and there was no rain. There was not enough food to eat anywhere in the country. The son was hungry and needed money. [15]So he got a job with one of the citizens there. The man sent the son into the fields to feed pigs. [16]The son was so hungry that he was willing to eat the food the pigs were eating. But no one gave him anything. [17]The son realized that he had been very foolish. He thought, 'All of my father's servants have plenty of food. But I am here, almost dying with hunger. [18]I will leave and return to my father. I'll say to him: Father, I have sinned against God and against you. [19]I am not good enough to be called your son. But let me be like one of your servants.' [20]So the son left and went to his father.

Do God's Word:

Sooner or later, everyone does something that they know they shouldn't do. That is called *sin*. The next time you do something wrong, if you will simply tell God about your sin and you are truly sorry, he will forgive you. He will wipe it all away—just as if it had never happened!

"While the son was still a long way off, his father saw him coming. He ran to him, and hugged and kissed him. ²²The father said to his servants, 'Hurry! Bring the best clothes and put them on him. ²³And get our fat calf and kill it. Then we can have a feast! ²⁴My son was lost, but now he is found!' So they began to celebrate.

²⁵"The older son heard the sound of music and dancing. ²⁸The older son was angry. So his father went out and begged him to come in. ²⁹The son said, 'I have always obeyed your commands. ³⁰But your other son has wasted all your money. Then he comes home, and you kill the fat calf for him!' ³¹The father said to him, 'Son, you are always with me. All that I have is yours. ³²We had to celebrate because your brother was lost, but now he is found.'"

Pray God's Word:

God, be merciful to me because you are loving. Because you are always ready to be merciful, wipe out all my wrongs. Wash away all my guilt and make me clean again. Create in me a pure heart, God. Make my spirit right again.

—Psalm 51:1–2, 10

The Cross

Selections from Mark 14, John 18, and Luke 23

[14:32]Jesus and his followers went to a place called Gethsemane. He said to his followers, "Sit here while I pray. [34]My heart is breaking with sadness. Stay here and watch."

[35]Jesus walked a little farther away. Then he fell on the ground and prayed. [36]He prayed, "Father! You can do all things. Let me not have this cup of suffering. But do what you want, not what I want."

[37]Then Jesus went back to his followers. He found them asleep. He said, "Why are you sleeping? [38]Stay awake and pray."

[39]Again Jesus went away and prayed the same thing. [40]Then he went back to the followers. Again he found them asleep because their eyes were very heavy.

[41]After Jesus prayed a third time, he went back to his followers. He said to them, "You are still sleeping? The time has come for the Son of Man to be given to sinful people. [42]Get up! We must go. Here comes the man who has turned against me."

Remember God's Word:
For God loved the world so much that he gave his only Son.
—JOHN 3:16

Judas knew where this place was, because Jesus met there often with his followers. Judas was the one who turned against Jesus. [3]So Judas led a group of soldiers to the garden. They were carrying torches, lanterns, and weapons.

[4]Jesus knew everything that would happen to him. Jesus went out and asked, "Who is it you are looking for?"

[5]The men answered, "Jesus from Nazareth."

Jesus said, "I am Jesus. [8]So if you are looking for me, then let these other men go."

[10]Simon Peter had a sword. He took out the sword and struck the servant of the high priest, cutting off his right ear. [11]Jesus said to Peter, "Put your sword back. Shall I not drink of the cup the Father has given me?"

[12]Then the soldiers with their commander and the Jewish guards arrested Jesus.

^{14:53}The people who arrested Jesus led him to the house of the high priest. ⁶¹The high priest asked Jesus: "Are you the Christ, the Son of God?"

⁶²Jesus answered, "I am."

⁶³When the high priest heard this, he was very angry. ⁶⁴They all said that Jesus should be killed.

^{23:1}Then the whole group stood up and led Jesus to Pilate. ³Pilate asked Jesus, "Are you the king of the Jews?"

Jesus answered, "Yes, that is right."

¹³Pilate called all the people together. ¹⁴He said to them, "I have not found him guilty. ¹⁵He has done nothing for which he should die."

¹⁸But all the people shouted, "Kill him! ²¹Kill him on a cross!"

²³Their yelling became so loud that ²⁵Pilate gave Jesus to them to be killed.

Pray God's Word:
Jesus gave himself for our sins to free us from this evil world we live in. The glory belongs to God forever and ever. Amen.
—GALATIANS 1:4–5

²⁶The soldiers led Jesus away. ³²There were also two criminals led out with Jesus to be killed. ³³The soldiers nailed Jesus to his cross. They also nailed the criminals to their crosses. ³⁴Jesus said, "Father, forgive them. They don't know what they are doing."

⁴⁴It was about noon, and the whole land became dark until three o'clock in the afternoon. ⁴⁶Jesus cried out in a loud voice, "Father, I give you my life." After Jesus said this, he died.

⁴⁸Many people had gathered there. When they saw what happened, they were so sad. ⁴⁹Those who were close friends of Jesus were there. Some were women. They all stood far away from the cross and watched.

⁵⁰⁻⁵¹A man from the Jewish town of Arimathea was there, too. His name was Joseph. He was a good, religious man. ⁵³Joseph took the body down from the cross and wrapped it in cloth. Then he put Jesus' body in a tomb that was cut in a wall of rock.

⁵⁵The women who had come from Galilee with Jesus followed Joseph. They saw the tomb and saw inside where the body of Jesus was laid. ⁵⁶Then the women left.

On the Sabbath day they rested, as the law of Moses commanded.

Do God's Word:

Jesus didn't have to go to the cross. He didn't want to go to the cross. But he did it anyway. He did it to save his people—to save you. That is called sacrifice.

You can thank Jesus with your own sacrifice—by giving up something that you want, or perhaps by doing something you would rather not. Could that money you've been saving help someone buy food? Could you take out the trash even when it's not your job? Could your toy bring a smile to a child who doesn't have any toys?

How can you thank Jesus?

Jesus Is Alive!

Selections from Luke 24

24:1Very early on the first day of the week, the women came to the tomb where Jesus' body was laid. 2They found that the stone had been rolled away from the entrance of the tomb. 3They went in, but they did not find the body of the Lord Jesus.

Do God's Word:

Jesus died, but then he was raised to life again. And when you believe in Jesus you can have a whole new life too.

As a symbol of new life, plant a "tomb garden." Put some dirt in a cup, filling it about halfway up. Sprinkle in some grass seeds. Add a little more dirt on top, shaping it into a mound—like a tomb. Add a small rock—like the one in front of Jesus' tomb. Then add a little water. Place your tomb garden in a sunny spot and wait to see the grass spring up into "new life"!

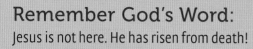

Remember God's Word:
Jesus is not here. He has risen from death!
—LUKE 24:6

142

⁴While they were wondering about this, two men in shining clothes suddenly stood beside them. ⁵The women were very afraid; they bowed their heads to the ground. The men said to the women, "Why are you looking for a living person here? This is a place for the dead. ⁶Jesus is not here. He has risen from death!"

⁹The women left the tomb and told all these things to the 11 apostles and the other followers. ¹⁰The women told the apostles everything that had happened at the tomb. ¹¹But they did not believe the women. It sounded like nonsense. ¹²But Peter got up and ran to the tomb. He looked in, but he saw only the cloth that Jesus' body had been wrapped in. Peter went away to be alone, wondering about what had happened.

Pray God's Word:
Lord, I look up to you.
You live in heaven.
You are very kind.
Be good to those who are good,
whose hearts are honest.
[And] Lord, give me life by your love.
—PSALM 123:1; 119:156; 125:4; 119:159

Jesus Goes Back Home—to Heaven

Selections from John 20 and Acts 1

[20:19]It was the first day of the week. That evening Jesus' followers were together. The doors were locked, because they were afraid of the Jews. Then Jesus came and stood among them. He said, "Peace be with you!" [20]After he said this, he showed them his hands and his side. The followers were very happy when they saw the Lord.

[24]Thomas was not with the followers when Jesus came. [25]The other followers told Thomas, "We saw the Lord."

But Thomas said, "I will not believe it until I see the nail marks in his hands. And I will not believe until I put my finger where the nails were and put my hand into his side."

[26]A week later the followers were in the house again. Thomas was with them. The doors were locked, but Jesus came in and stood among them. [27]He said to Thomas, "Put your finger here. Look at my hands. Put your hand here in my side. Stop doubting and believe."

[28]Thomas said to him, "My Lord and my God!"

[29]Then Jesus told him, "You believe because you see me. Those who believe without seeing me will be truly happy."

Pray God's Word:
Lord, you have made me happy by what you have done.
I will sing for joy about what your hands have done.
—Psalm 92:4

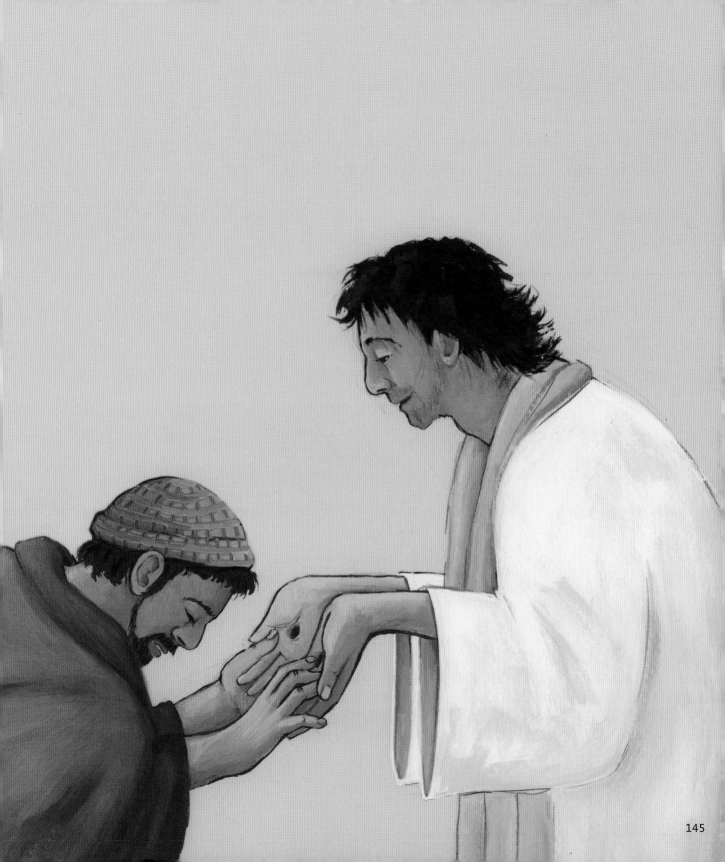

¹:³After his death, he proved in many ways that he was alive. The apostles saw Jesus during the 40 days after he was raised from death. He spoke to them about the kingdom of God.

⁷Jesus said to them, ⁸"The Holy Spirit will come to you. Then you will receive power. You will be my witnesses in every part of the world."

⁹After he said this, as they were watching, he was lifted up. A cloud hid him from their sight. ¹⁰As he was going, they were looking into the sky. Suddenly, two men wearing white clothes stood beside them. ¹¹They said, "Men of Galilee, why are you standing here looking into the sky? You saw Jesus taken away from you into heaven. He will come back in the same way you saw him go."

Remember God's Word:
Jesus Christ is Lord.
—PHILIPPIANS 2:11

Do God's Word:

Jesus wanted his followers to tell all the world about him—to be a witness. He wants you to be a witness too. But you don't have to travel all over the world to be a witness. You can witness right where you are.

Who can you tell about Jesus? At school? At the playground? Or at practice? How many people can you find to tell about Jesus?

The Holy Spirit Comes to Earth

Selections from Acts 1 and 2

[1:6]The apostles were all together.

[2:1]When the day of Pentecost came, they were all in one place. [2]Suddenly a noise came from heaven. It sounded like a strong wind blowing. This noise filled the whole house where they were sitting. [3]They saw something that looked like flames of fire. The flames were separated and stood over each person there. [4]They were all filled with the Holy Spirit, and they began to speak different languages.

[5]There were some Jews staying in Jerusalem who were from every country in the world. [6]When they heard this noise, [7]they were completely amazed. They said, "Aren't all these men that we hear speaking from Galilee? [8]But each of us hears them in his own language. How is this possible?"

Do God's Word:

Take a balloon. Before it is blown up, it is very small. You can't do much with it. Now blow it up. It's the same color on the outside, but now it is much bigger—because of what is inside it. In the same way, when you accept Jesus, the Holy Spirit fills you up and makes you bigger—and stronger—than you are on your own.

[14]Peter stood up with the 11 apostles. In a loud voice he spoke to the crowd:

[22]"Listen to these words: Jesus from Nazareth was a very special man. God clearly showed this to you by the miracles, wonders, and signs God did through him. [23]Jesus was given to you, and you killed him. But God knew all this would happen. This was God's plan which he had made long ago. [24]God raised Jesus from death. Death could not hold him.

[36]"So, all the people of Israel should know this truly: God has made Jesus both Lord and Christ. He is the man you nailed to the cross!"

[37]When the people heard this, they were sick at heart. They asked Peter and the other apostles, "What shall we do?"

[38]Peter said to them, "Change your hearts and lives and be baptized in the name of Jesus Christ for the forgiveness of your sins. And you will receive the gift of the Holy Spirit."

[41]Then those people who accepted what Peter said were baptized. About 3,000 people were added to the number of believers that day.

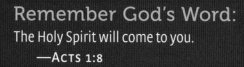

Remember God's Word:
The Holy Spirit will come to you.
—Acts 1:8

Pray God's Word:
Lord, tell me your ways.
Show me how to live.
Guide me in your truth.
Teach me, my God, my Savior.
I trust you all day long.
—Psalm 25:4–5

Saul's Change of Heart

Selections from Acts 9, 21, 23, 27, and 28, and Philippians 1

^{9:1}In Jerusalem Saul was trying to frighten the followers of the Lord by saying he would kill them. ²Saul wanted to find people in Damascus who were followers of Christ's Way. If he found any, he would arrest them and bring them back to Jerusalem.

³So Saul went to Damascus. As he came near the city, a bright light from heaven suddenly flashed around him. ⁴Saul fell to the ground. He heard a voice saying to him, "Saul, Saul! Why are you doing things against me?"

⁵Saul said, "Who are you, Lord?"

The voice answered, "I am Jesus. I am the One you are trying to hurt. ⁶Get up now and go into the city. Someone there will tell you what you must do."

⁸Saul opened his eyes, but he could not see. So the men with Saul led him into Damascus. ⁹For three days Saul could not see, and he did not eat or drink.

¹⁰There was a follower of Jesus in Damascus named Ananias. The Lord spoke to Ananias in a vision, "Ananias! ¹¹Get up and go to Saul."

¹³But Ananias answered, "Lord, many people have told me about the terrible things he did to your people in Jerusalem."

¹⁵But the Lord said, "Go! I have chosen Saul for an important work."

¹⁷So Ananias went. He laid his hands on Saul and said, "The Lord Jesus sent me so that you can see again and be filled with the Holy Spirit." ¹⁸Immediately, something that looked like fish scales fell from Saul's eyes. He was able to see again! Then Saul got up and was baptized.

²⁸Saul went everywhere in Jerusalem, preaching boldly in the name of Jesus. ²⁹He would often talk and argue with the Jews. But they were trying to kill him. ³⁰When the brothers learned about this, they took Saul to Caesarea.

Saul, also called Paul, traveled to many different places. Everywhere he went, he spoke boldly for God, preaching the Good News in the synagogues. Then, one day, Paul returned to Jerusalem.

Do God's Word:

While Paul was in prison, he wrote many letters. His letters encouraged the followers of Christ to keep believing and to live right.

Lots of people today need encouragement also. Do you know someone who isn't feeling well? Or someone who is feeling sad? Write a cheerful note or draw a picture encouraging that person. Ask your parents to help you mail it. You'll bring a smile to your friend's day—and to God's day too!

^{21:27}Some Jews from Asia saw Paul at the Temple. They grabbed Paul. ²⁸They shouted, "This is the man who goes everywhere teaching things that are against the law of Moses, against our people, and against this Temple."

³⁰They took Paul and dragged him out of the Temple. ³¹The people were about to kill Paul. Now the commander of the Roman army in Jerusalem learned that there was trouble. ³³The commander went to Paul and arrested him ^{23:10}and put him in the army building.

¹¹The next night the Lord came and stood by Paul. He said, "Be brave! You have told people in Jerusalem about me. You must do the same in Rome also."
^{27:1}It was decided that [Paul] would sail for Italy.
^{28:16}[He] arrived at Rome.

While Paul was in prison, he wrote many letters to the believers. Here is one of them.

1:1To all of God's holy people in Christ Jesus.

2Grace and peace to you from God our Father and the Lord Jesus Christ.

9This is my prayer for you: that your love will grow more and more; 10that you will see the difference between good and bad and choose the good.

12I want you to know that what has happened to me has helped to spread the Good News. 13I am in prison because I am a believer in Christ.

20The thing I want and hope for is that I will not fail Christ in anything. 21To me the only important thing about living is Christ.

27Be sure that you live in a way that brings honor to the Good News of Christ.

Remember God's Word:
The followers were filled with joy and the Holy Spirit.
—ACTS 13:52

Pray God's Word:
Lord, we are your servants.
Help us to speak your word without fear.
—ACTS 4:29

A Peek into Heaven

Selections from Revelation 1, 4, and 21–22

1:4 From John,

10 On the Lord's day, I heard a loud voice behind me that sounded like a trumpet.

4:1 I looked, and there before me was an open door in heaven. And I heard the voice that sounded like a trumpet. The voice said, "Come up here, and I will show you what must happen after this." **2** Then the Spirit took control of me. There before me was a throne in heaven. Someone was sitting on the throne. **3** The One who sat on the throne looked like precious stones, like jasper and carnelian. All around the throne was a rainbow the color of an emerald. **4** Around the throne there were 24 other thrones. There were 24 elders sitting on the 24 thrones. The elders were dressed in white, and they had golden crowns on their heads. **5** Lightning flashes and noises of thunder came from the throne. **6** Also before the throne there was something that looked like a sea of glass. It was clear like crystal.

Around the throne, on each side, there were four living things. **8** Day and night they never stop saying:

"Holy, holy, holy is the Lord God All-Powerful.

He was, he is, and he is coming."

9 These living things give glory and honor and thanks to the One who sits on the throne. He is the One who lives forever and ever.

Remember God's Word:
He will wipe away every tear from their eyes. There will be no more death, sadness, crying, or pain.
— REVELATION 21:4

²¹:¹Then I saw a new heaven and a new earth. The first heaven and the first earth had disappeared. ²And I saw the holy city coming down out of heaven from God. This holy city is the new Jerusalem. ³I heard a loud voice from the throne. The voice said, "Now God's home is with men. He will live with them, and they will be his people. God himself will be with them and will be their God. ⁴He will wipe away every tear from their eyes. There will be no more death, sadness, crying, or pain. All the old ways are gone."

⁵The One who was sitting on the throne said, "Look! I am making everything new!"

²²:²¹The grace of the Lord Jesus be with all. Amen.

Do God's Word:

No more tears. No more death or sadness or pain. What a wonderful place heaven will be! As you go through your day, notice all the things that will *not* be needed in heaven. No tissues, because there will be no more tears. No more hospitals, because there will be no sickness. No more bandages, because there will be no more pain. How many things can you find that you *won't* need in heaven?

Pray God's Word:

God, examine me and know my heart.
Test me and know my thoughts.
See if there is any bad thing in me.
Lead me in the way you set long ago.
—PSALM 139:23–24

161

The Ten Commandments

I. YOU MUST NOT HAVE ANY OTHER GODS EXCEPT ME.

II. YOU MUST NOT MAKE FOR YOURSELVES ANY IDOLS. YOU MUST NOT WORSHIP OR SERVE ANY IDOL.

III. YOU MUST NOT USE THE NAME OF THE LORD YOUR GOD THOUGHTLESSLY.

IV. REMEMBER TO KEEP THE SABBATH AS A HOLY DAY.

V. HONOR YOUR FATHER AND YOUR MOTHER.

VI. YOU MUST NOT MURDER ANYONE.

VII. YOU MUST NOT BE GUILTY OF ADULTERY.

VIII. YOU MUST NOT STEAL.

IX. YOU MUST NOT TELL LIES ABOUT YOUR NEIGHBOR IN COURT.

X. YOU MUST NOT WANT TO TAKE ANYTHING THAT BELONGS TO YOUR NEIGHBOR.

David wrote many songs and poems praising the Lord. They are found in the book of Psalms. The Twenty-Third Psalm tells of David's trust in the Lord. You can trust God too. God will take care of you, just as he took care of David.

The Twenty-Third Psalm

The Lord is my shepherd.
I have everything I need.
[2]He gives me rest in green pastures.
He leads me to calm water.
[3]He gives me new strength.
For the good of his name,
he leads me on paths that are right.
[4]Even if I walk
through a very dark valley,
I will not be afraid
because you are with me.
Your rod and your walking stick comfort me.
[5]You prepare a meal for me
in front of my enemies.
You pour oil of blessing on my head.
You give me more than I can hold.
[6]Surely your goodness and love will be with me
all my life.
And I will live in the house of the Lord forever.

Selected Verses from the Book of Proverbs

My child, sinners will try to lead you into sin.
But do not follow them.
—PROVERBS 1:10

Remember the Lord in everything you do.
And he will give you success.
—PROVERBS 3:6

Whenever you are able,
do good to people who need help.
—PROVERBS 3:27

Always remember what you have been taught.
Don't let go of it.
Keep safe all that you have learned.
It is the most important thing in your life.
—PROVERBS 4:13

Don't use your mouth to tell lies.
Don't ever say things that are not true.
   —Proverbs 4:24

Hatred stirs up trouble.
But love forgives all wrongs.
   —Proverbs 10:12

A person who quickly gets angry causes trouble.
But a person who controls his temper stops a quarrel.
   —Proverbs 15:18

Even a child is known by his behavior.
His actions show if he is innocent and good.
   —Proverbs 20:11

A person who is careful about what he says
keeps himself out of trouble.
   —Proverbs 21:23

Every word of God can be trusted.
He protects those who come to him for safety.
   —Proverbs 30:5

Mary Praises God (Mary's Song)

Luke 1:46–55

⁴⁶Then Mary said,
"My soul praises the Lord;
⁴⁷my heart is happy because God is my Savior.
⁴⁸I am not important, but God has shown his care for me, his servant girl.
From now on, all people will say that I am blessed,
⁴⁹because the Powerful One has done great things for me.
His name is holy.
⁵⁰God will always give mercy
to those who worship him.
⁵¹God's arm is strong.
He scatters the people who are proud
and think great things about themselves.
⁵²God brings down rulers from their thrones,
and he raises up the humble.
⁵³God fills the hungry with good things,
but he sends the rich away with nothing.
⁵⁴God has helped his people Israel who serve him.
He gave them his mercy.
⁵⁵God has done what he promised to our ancestors,
to Abraham and to his children forever."

The Lord's Prayer

Matthew 6:9–13

[9]When you pray, you should pray like this:
"Our Father in heaven,
we pray that your name will always be kept holy.
[10]We pray that your kingdom will come.
We pray that what you want will be done,
here on earth as it is in heaven.
[11]Give us the food we need for each day.
[12]Forgive the sins we have done,
just as we have forgiven those who did wrong to us.
[13]Do not cause us to be tested;
but save us from the Evil One."

MY READING CHART

Stories from the Old Testament

DATE READ	TITLE
_____	○ The Beginning of the World
_____	○ The Very First Sin
_____	○ Noah and the Great Flood
_____	○ A Tower Called "Babel"
_____	○ God Makes a Promise
_____	○ Joseph and His Brothers
_____	○ Moses and the Stubborn King
_____	○ Rahab and the Spies
_____	○ The Story of Ruth
_____	○ Hannah's Special Baby
_____	○ David and the Great Big Giant
_____	○ Nehemiah and the Broken-Down Wall
_____	○ Daniel and the Lions

Stories of the New Testament

DATE READ   TITLE

_____   ○ Jesus Is Born!

_____   ○ The Boy Jesus in the Temple

_____   ○ Jesus Teaches the People

_____   ○ Zacchaeus, the Wee Little Man

_____   ○ Two Miracles

_____   ○ A Miracle for Dinner

_____   ○ A Runaway Boy Comes Home

_____   ○ The Cross

_____   ○ Jesus Is Alive!

_____   ○ Jesus Goes Back Home—to Heaven

_____   ○ The Holy Spirit Comes to Earth

_____   ○ Saul's Change of Heart

_____   ○ A Peek into Heaven

The Twelve Apostles

Peter

James, son of Zebedee

John

Andrew

Philip

Bartholomew

Matthew

Thomas

James, son of Alphaeus

Thaddaeus

Simon the Zealot

Judas Iscariot

John and James, son of Zebedee, were brothers. Jesus gave them the name of Boanerges, which means "Sons of Thunder." Jesus also gave Peter his name (he was named Simon before). Bartholomew was also known as Nathanael. After Judas betrayed Jesus, a new apostle named Matthias joined the group.

The Twelve Tribes of Israel

Asher

Benjamin

Dan

Gad

Issachar

Joseph

Judah

Levi

Naphtali

Reuben

Simeon

Zebulun

Sometimes the twelve tribes of Israel are listed differently. For example, sometimes Joseph, Reuben, Dan, or Levi may not be listed. Sometimes Ephraim or Manasseh is listed in the place of another tribe. But there are always twelve tribes.

SONGS ABOUT JESUS

Jesus Loves Me

Jesus loves me! This I know,
For the Bible tells me so.
Little ones to Him belong;
They are weak, but He is strong.

Yes, Jesus loves me!
Yes, Jesus loves me!
Yes, Jesus loves me!
The Bible tells me so.

Words by Anna B. Warner

Jesus Loves the Little Children

Jesus loves the little children,
All the children of the world.
Red and yellow, black and white,
All are precious in His sight.
Jesus loves the little children of the world.

Words by C. Herbert Woolston

BOOKS OF THE BIBLE
Old Testament

Genesis	Psalms
Exodus	Proverbs
Leviticus	Ecclesiastes
Numbers	Song of Solomon
Deuteronomy	Isaiah
Joshua	Jeremiah
Judges	Lamentations
Ruth	Ezekiel
1 Samuel	Daniel
2 Samuel	Hosea
1 Kings	Joel
2 Kings	Amos
1 Chronicles	Obadiah
2 Chronicles	Jonah
Ezra	Micah
Nehemiah	Nahum
Esther	Habakkuk
Job	Zephaniah
	Haggai
	Zechariah
	Malachi

New Testament

Matthew

Mark

Luke

John

Acts

Romans

1 Corinthians

2 Corinthians

Galatians

Ephesians

Philippians

Colossians

1 Thessalonians

2 Thessalonians

1 Timothy

2 Timothy

Titus

Philemon

Hebrews

James

1 Peter

2 Peter

1 John

2 John

3 John

Jude

Revelation

MY MEMORY VERSE CHART
Verses from the Old Testament

DATE MEMORIZED		VERSE
_____	○	God looked at everything he had made, and it was very good. Genesis 1:31
_____	○	The Lord God put the man in the garden of Eden to care for it and work it. Genesis 2:15
_____	○	"I am putting my rainbow in the clouds." Genesis 9:13
_____	○	Don't say, "I'll pay you back for the evil you did." Wait for the Lord. He will make things right. Proverbs 20:22
_____	○	The Lord says, "I will make you wise. I will show you where to go. I will guide you and watch over you." Psalm 32:8
_____	○	The Lord your God will be with you everywhere you go. Joshua 1:9
_____	○	I will pray to the Lord. And he will answer me. Psalm 3:4
_____	○	David defeated the Philistine with only a sling and a stone! 1 Samuel 17:50
_____	○	First I prayed to the God of heaven. Nehemiah 2:4
_____	○	The Lord is my light and the one who saves me. Psalm 27:1

Verses from the New Testament

DATE MEMORIZED		VERSE
_____	○	Go and make followers of all people in the world. Matthew 28:19
_____	○	Every good action and every perfect gift is from God. James 1:17
_____	○	Then the King will answer, "I tell you the truth. Anything you did for any of my people here, you also did for me." Matthew 25:40
_____	○	Today your Savior was born in David's town. He is Christ, the Lord. Luke 2:11
_____	○	Jesus continued to learn more and more and to grow physically. People liked him, and he pleased God. Luke 2:52
_____	○	But I tell you, love your enemies. Pray for those who hurt you. Matthew 5:44
_____	○	The Son of Man came to find lost people and save them. Luke 19:10
_____	○	Don't be afraid; only believe. Mark 5:36
_____	○	Jesus looked up to heaven and thanked God for the bread. Mark 6:41
_____	○	Come back to God, and he will forgive your sins. Acts 3:19
_____	○	For God loved the world so much that he gave his only Son. John 3:16
_____	○	Jesus is not here. He has risen from death! Luke 24:6
_____	○	Jesus Christ is Lord. Philippians 2:11
_____	○	The Holy Spirit will come to you. Acts 1:8
_____	○	The followers were filled with joy and the Holy Spirit. Acts 13:52
_____	○	He will wipe away every tear from their eyes. There will be no more death, sadness, crying, or pain. Revelation 21:4

If you want to know more about how to live for Jesus,
talk to your parents or a trusted minister.
And talk to God and read the Bible every day.
God will help you and be with you!